HOW CAN I EXPERIMENT WITH ... ?

A PULLEY

David and Patricia Armentrout

Rourke
Publishing LLC
Vero Beach, Florida 32964

www.rourkepublishing.com

PHOTO CREDITS: ©Armentrout Cover, pg 11; ©James P. Rowan pg 4; ©David French Photography pgs 14, 17, 20, 23, 27, 29; ©Painet, Inc. pgs 7, 9, 19, 25; ©Mary Kate Denny/PhotoEdit/PictureQuest pg 13.

Cover: *Compound bows have pulleys to reduce the effort of pulling the bow.*

Editor: Frank Sloan

Cover design: Nicola Stratford

Series Consulting Editor: Henry Rasof, a former editor with Franklin Watts, has edited many science books for children and young adults.

Library of Congress Cataloging-in-Publication Data

Armentrout, David, 1962-
  How can I experiment with simple machines? A pulley / David and
Patricia Armentrout.
        p. cm.
Summary: Defines pulleys, explains their functions, and suggests simple
experiments to demonstrate how they work.
Includes bibliographical references and index.
  ISBN 1-58952-335-0
  1. Pulleys—Juvenile literature. [1. Pulleys--Experiments. 2.
Experiments.] I. Title: Pulley. II. Armentrout, Patricia, 1960- III.
Title.
  TJ1103 .A758 2002
  621.8—dc21
                                                            2002007652

Printed in the USA

w/w

Table of Contents

Pulley (PUL ee) — a wheel, usually grooved, that holds a rope or cable; a simple machine that makes work easier

Some pulleys have more than one wheel and cable.

Simple Machines

The wheel, the lever, and the inclined plane are simple machines. The wheel helps us move objects with less **friction**. The lever helps us move objects with less effort. The inclined plane helps us move objects to different levels.

The wedge, the screw, and the pulley are simple machines, too. The wedge acts like a moving inclined plane. The screw is a **spiraling** inclined plane. Machines with pulleys can lift heavy loads.

A bicycle is made up of several simple machines. Can you see any simple machines here?

Using Machines

Did you know that when you close the lid of a pickle jar you are using a simple machine? You are using a screw. How about when you use a bottle opener to remove a bottle cap? A bottle opener is a type of lever.

Have you ever watched a crane lift a heavy load? Cranes use pulleys to make the job easier. Cranes that have a combination of pulleys give a **mechanical advantage**. Mechanical advantage is what you gain when a machine allows you to use less force, or effort.

A truck crane with a movable pulley can lift and move a silo.

Pulleys and Work

There are two types of pulleys—fixed and movable. A fixed pulley stays in place. A movable pulley moves with the load. What do pulleys have to do with work? Well, first you need to know what work is. Work is the force used to move an object over a distance.

Scientists use the formula:

FORCE x DISTANCE = WORK

When you combine a fixed pulley with a movable pulley, the pulley system allows you to use less force to get the work done.

A fixed pulley allows you to change the direction of the force.

Fixed Pulley

A fixed pulley does not give you a mechanical advantage, but it does allow you to change the direction of the force.

A flagpole has a fixed pulley at the top of the pole. Think about what happens when you use a pulley to raise a flag. When you pull down on one side of the rope, the flag attached to the other side of the rope goes up. Most people would agree that it's easier to raise a flag using a pulley than it is to climb a ladder to the top of the flagpole.

It's easy to raise a flag when a pulley is attached to the top of the pole.

14 *Make a fixed pulley with a broom handle, a bucket, and a piece of string.*

Make a Fixed Pulley

You will need:

- 2 chairs with open backs
- broom
- friend
- scissors
- string
- small bucket with handle
- coins for weight

Place the two chairs back to back 3 feet (1m) apart. Put the broom handle between the chair backs forming a bar. Have your friend hold the broom steady. Use the scissors to cut a length of the string twice the distance from the broom handle to the floor. Use one end of the string to tie a knot around the handle of the bucket. Put the bucket on the floor under the broom handle. Put some coins in the bucket for weight. Place the free end of the string up and over the broom handle. The broom handle acts as your pulley.

15

Experiment with Your Fixed Pulley

Sit in front of the pulley and pull down on the free end of the string. Notice the distance the string is pulled and the distance the load is raised. When you use a fixed pulley, the load moves the same distance as the pull. The force needed to lift the load equals the weight of the load.

This experiment will help you learn how a fixed pulley works.

Pulleys and Counterweights

An elevator is a machine that uses a fixed pulley system. The elevator car is raised or lowered by a cable that runs up and over a pulley at the top of the shaft. The other end of the cable is attached to a **counterweight**. The counterweight balances the weight of the car. The motor that turns the pulley needs only enough power to lift the weight of the passengers and not the weight of the car.

Tower cranes used in skyscraper construction have pulleys with counterweights. Can you think of any other machines that use pulleys and counterweights?

A counterweight must balance the weight of the tower crane as it lifts its heavy load.

A paper clip slides freely on a string and acts as a movable pulley.

Make a Movable Pulley

A movable pulley is a pulley that is able to move with the load. To make a movable pulley, you will need all the materials from the first experiment (page 15) plus a paper clip.

Place the chairs and the broom the same way you did in the first experiment. Have your friend hold the broom handle steady. Use the scissors to cut a length of string twice the distance from the broom handle to the floor. Use one end of the string to tie a knot around the broom handle.

Open the paper clip to form a hook at each end. Hold up the free end of the string. Place one hook of the paper clip on the string. The paper clip should slide freely when you raise and lower the string. The paper clip acts as your movable pulley.

Experiment with Your Movable Pulley

Your friend will need a yardstick for this experiment with the movable pulley you just made.

Your movable pulley allows each half of the string to support half the weight of the load. In other words, the half of the string from the broom handle to the paper clip shares the weight of the load equally with the half of the string from the paper clip to your hand.

Place the bucket, with coins inside, on the floor under the broom handle. Set the handle of the bucket on the lower hook of the paper clip. Lift the string up until the bucket rises 10 inches (25 cm) from the floor. Have your friend measure 10 inches (25 cm) with the yardstick. It should take 20 inches (about 51 cm) of string to lift the bucket 10 inches (25 cm).

Your movable pulley allows you to use half the effort at twice the distance.

A movable pulley allows you to use less effort.

Pulleys Working with Pulleys

Some machines, like cranes, move big loads. Cranes lift heavy loads by using more than one pulley at one time. Cranes often use pulley systems called block and tackle. Block and tackle has several movable pulleys that reduce the amount of force needed to move the load.

You now know that a fixed pulley allows for change in direction, and a movable pulley allows you to share the weight of the load. Let's see what happens when you combine a fixed pulley with a movable pulley.

Rigging on ships can consist of several fixed and movable pulleys. Pulleys are used to raise and lower sails on ships.

Make a Double Pulley System

You will use all the materials from the last experiment (page 22) except the paper clip.

Place the chairs and the broom the same way you did in the last experiment. Have your friend hold the broom handle steady. Using the scissors, cut a length of string three times the distance from the broom handle to the floor. Use one end of the string to tie a knot around the broom handle. Place the bucket on the floor below the string. Pass the free end of the string through the bucket handle and then up and over the broom handle.

Your fixed pulley is located at the broom handle. Your movable pulley is the bucket handle that moves freely when the string is raised and lowered.

It is easier to lift a load using a double pulley system.

Experiment with Your Double Pulley System

   Put some coins in the bucket for weight. Pull down on the free end of the string until the bucket rises 10 inches (25 cm) from the floor. Have your friend measure 10 inches (25 cm) with the yardstick. How much string did it take to raise the bucket? Did it take 20 inches (about 51 cm)? Your double pulley system gave you the benefit of change in direction as well as the mechanical advantage of sharing the weight of the load.

A double pulley system gives you a mechanical advantage.

Glossary

counterweight (KOUN ter wayt) — a weight
that balances the weight of a load

friction (FRIK shun) — a force that slows
two objects when they are rubbed together

mechanical advantage (mi KAN eh kul
ad VAN tij) — what you gain when a
simple machine allows you to use
less effort

spiraling (SPY ruh ling) — coiling around

Further Reading

Macaulay, David. *The New Way Things Work.*
Houghton Mifflin Company, 1998
Seller, Mick. *Wheels, Pulleys & Levers.*
Gloucester Press, 1993
VanCleave, Janice. *Machines.* John Wiley &
Sons, Inc., 1993

Websites to Visit

http://www.kidskonnect.com/SimpleMachines/
SimpleMachinesHome.html
http://www.mos.org/sin/Leonardo/
InventorsToolbox.html
http://www.brainpop.com/tech/simplemachines/

Index

About the Authors

David and Patricia Armentrout have written many nonfiction books for young readers. They specialize in science and social studies topics. They have had several books published for primary school reading. The Armentrouts live in Cincinnati, Ohio, with their two children.